The Mystery of the Missing Book

D0970855

Natalie West
Illustrated by Eva Vagreti Cockrille

Rigby®

Level O Guided Reading Chapter Book

On Our Way to English: *The Mystery of the Missing Book*

© 2004 by Rigby
1000 Hart Road
Barrington, IL 60010
www.rigby.com

Text by Natalie West
Illustrated by Eva Vagreti Cockrille

09 08 07 06 05 04
10 9 8 7 6 5 4 3

Printed in China

ISBN 0-7578-4510-X

Contents

Chapter 1

The Newspaper

Julia Demos couldn't wait to find out what would happen next. In just another moment or two, she would be able to guess who the criminal was! As she was turning the page of her mystery book, the school bell rang.

Ms. Smith, Julia's teacher, asked all of the students to put away whatever they were doing, but Julia kept reading. She couldn't stop now that she was at the best part of the book!

"Julia, it's time to pay attention, so please put down your book."

"Sorry, Ms. Smith," Julia said, quickly shutting her book and placing it inside her desk.

"I have a new project to tell you about," said Ms. Smith. "Our class is going to start a school newspaper, and each of you will be responsible for a different section of the paper."

Julia and her classmates became excited as Ms. Smith gave each of them their newspaper assignment. Gladys, Julia's best friend, would write a column about events happening around the school, and Julia would write the newspaper's advice column.

During lunch Julia and Gladys always sat with their friends. Today they discussed their new jobs.

"Ms. Smith always thinks of the best projects," Gladys said.

"Since I'm the sports writer, I'm going to go watch the soccer team practice tomorrow morning before school. What are you two going to write about?" Peter asked Julia.

"Until someone writes me a letter, I won't be able to write my advice column," Julia pointed out. "I hope someone will need help soon."

"I'm sure someone will need your help—like me, for instance," said Gladys, laughing. "You can give me advice on what I should write *my* column about."

"Oh, don't worry," Julia told her. "I'm sure that something interesting will happen for you to write about."

Chapter 2

How Can Julia Help?

That night Julia told her family about her new advice column. She was sure they could give her lots of helpful hints about writing it.

"What a fantastic idea!" said her mother.

"You'll be great at writing an advice column because you're so good at helping people," Julia's grandmother added.

"But how will I get people to write to me so that I can give them my advice?" asked Julia. "The newspaper is for the whole school, but only the people in my class know about it."

"I'd be happy to help you make some posters to advertise your column," suggested Teresa, Julia's older sister. "Tomorrow before school starts, you can hang them up in the hallways."

Happily, Julia accepted her sister's help. "Thanks, Teresa!

The next morning, Julia went to school early to hang up her posters. As she was hanging up the last poster, the school principal walked up behind her.

"Here, Julia, let me help you with that," Mr. Chan said, setting down his briefcase on the floor. He held the top of the poster to the wall for her while she taped it.

"Thanks, Mr. Chan," Julia said, turning to go to class. "You can write to me if you ever need advice."

Julia walked into the room as everyone was sitting down. She said good morning to Gladys, who was busy shutting the window because papers were being blown off the desks. Julia couldn't wait to get back to her mystery book because she hadn't had any time to finish reading it yesterday.

Ms. Smith was opening all of the drawers as if she was frantically searching for something.

"I'm sorry, but I can't find the book that I had planned to read to you today. It's one of my favorites. I've had it since I was about your age, and it's very special to me. I'm sure it was on my desk yesterday afternoon, but now it's missing!"

Julia listened carefully as Ms. Smith described the book to her students. "It is a ten-chapter book with a red cover." Maybe Julia could solve the mystery, just like the detective in the book she was reading!

Chapter 3

Worried Witness

After lunch the next day, Ms. Smith called Julia to her desk and said, "I found this envelope and it's addressed to the 'advice column girl.' I think it might be your very first letter asking for advice."

Julia quickly returned to her desk and opened the letter.

Dear Julia,

I think I might know who took Ms. Smith's book. I saw something that I shouldn't have seen, and I'm afraid I'll get in trouble if I tell. What do you think I should do? I want Ms. Smith to get her book back, but I don't want to get in trouble.

Signed,
Worried Witness

After school Julia showed the letter to Gladys and exclaimed, "This is great! Now I have a *real* mystery to solve!"

"Better yet," Gladys added, "now I'll have something interesting to write about for my column!"

Julia and Gladys spent so much time discussing who could have written the mysterious letter that they almost missed their bus. They had to get home quickly because the deadline for their stories was the next day. Ms. Smith was going to put the entire newspaper together on her home computer the next night. Then the following morning, the newspapers would be delivered to every class in school.

When she got home, Julia thought very hard about what advice to give Worried Witness. Should she tell this person to try to trap the thief or go straight to the police? Just then Teresa walked into the room.

"Teresa, you're just the person I wanted to see. I need your help with my advice column," said Julia. She told Teresa about the missing book and the letter she had received.

"I don't know whether to tell Worried Witness to try to catch the thief or to go to the police," she said.

"I don't think you should advise Worried Witness to do either of those things."

Working together, the two sisters came up with advice that they both liked.

Dear Worried Witness,
My advice to you is to wait until you have all of the facts. Don't do anything careless and don't accuse someone until you know the whole truth. Gather more clues and then report what you know.
Signed,
Julia

Chapter 4

Following the Clues

Julia wished that she could figure out who had written the letter to her. Then maybe she'd be closer to finding out who stole the book. The next day, Julia shared her problem with Gladys, saying, "I need to know who wrote this letter. Does this handwriting look familiar to you?"

"Worried Witness has to be in our class because no one else knows about Ms. Smith's book being stolen yet," Gladys said.

Dear Julia,

I think I might know who took Ms. Smith's book. I saw something that I shouldn't have seen, and I'm afraid I'll get in trouble if I tell. What do you think I should do? I want Ms. Smith to get her book back, but I don't want to get in trouble.

Signed,
Worried Witness

"You should get a handwriting sample from each person in our class so you can study the samples and compare them with the letter."

"Gladys, how can I ever repay you?" asked Julia. (Gladys always had the best ideas.)

"You can tell me what you discover about the missing book, and let me write about it in my newspaper column," joked Gladys.

23

Julia spent the rest of the day cleverly getting handwriting samples from her classmates. First she created a fake petition against bad cafeteria food, and many of her classmates signed it! Then she made get-well cards for Kim and Peter, two of her classmates who weren't in school that day. Everyone signed the cards, even Ms. Smith.

Gladys helped Julia by talking to Ms. Smith about possible suspects. Unfortunately, Ms. Smith didn't know who would want her book.

That night Julia compared her classmates' handwriting with the person who wrote the letter. But even with all of these samples, Julia didn't find a match. Disappointed that she couldn't solve the case, Julia went to bed.

The girls still hadn't given up hope the next morning because soon everyone would be reading the fifth-grade newspaper. Both girls were sure that Julia's advice column and Gladys's article about the missing book would help solve the mystery. People would probably talk about the stolen book, and maybe someone would remember something.

That afternoon Julia found a letter slipped inside the mystery book sitting on top of her desk. The handwriting of this letter exactly matched the handwriting of the first letter.

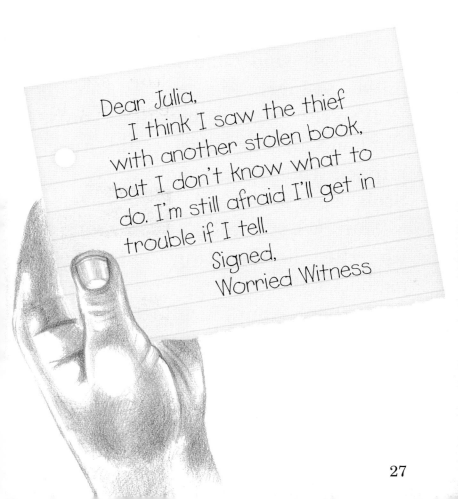

Dear Julia,
I think I saw the thief with another stolen book, but I don't know what to do. I'm still afraid I'll get in trouble if I tell.
Signed,
Worried Witness

Chapter 5

The Case Is Solved!

"**T**he letter writer must be in our class," said Gladys as she and Julia ate lunch.

"You're right because only someone in our class could have slipped the second note into my book," said Julia.

"But why couldn't you match up the handwriting samples?" asked Gladys.

"Maybe our collection of handwriting samples is incomplete," said Julia.

"I thought you got samples from everyone."

Suddenly Julia remembered something. "I think I know who wrote the letter! Worried Witness was home sick yesterday."

"Well, Kim was out yesterday, but she's still not back. She couldn't have written today's note."

"Peter was out yesterday, too, but he *is* back today," said Julia. "Maybe he gave me the second letter."

"Let's get a sample of his handwriting to see if he did it!" exclaimed Gladys. "We want to be sure before we accuse him. We don't want to be incorrect."

Back in the classroom, Gladys turned to her right and asked Peter if she could look at his homework so that she could compare her answers to his. She and Julia checked his handwriting, and it matched perfectly!

"Peter, I know you are Worried Witness," Julia whispered. "I can help you if you tell me who stole the book."

Peter thought for a minute. Then he said, "Well, I saw the thief leaving the classroom as I came to class early that morning after watching the soccer team practice. But I'm afraid to tell because the thief is . . ."

Just then Mr. Chan walked into the classroom, holding up a book. "I came to return this, Ms. Smith. It seems that this book has been causing a lot of confusion."

"Mr. Chan, I thought that my book was lost forever!" exclaimed Ms. Smith.

31

"I read your class newspaper," Mr. Chan explained, "and found out that I was a thief! Actually, when I borrowed the book, I left you a note, but it must have blown off your desk. I always leave a note when I borrow something from a teacher."

"Next time you'll have to write the note on the board so that it can't blow away," said Ms. Smith.

Julia, Gladys, and Peter smiled, happy that the mystery of the missing book had been solved.